HAZARDS OF NUCLEAR POWER

Hazards
of
Nuclear Power

by

Alan Roberts and Zhores Medvedev

Spokesman

First published in 1977

Cloth ISBN 0 85124 211 1
Paper ISBN 0 85124 212 X

Published by Spokesman
Bertrand Russell House, Gamble Street, Nottingham
Printed by the Russell Press Ltd., Nottingham

Contents

I   The Politics of Nuclear Energy   7
      Alan Roberts

II   Nuclear Disaster in the Soviet Union   58
      Zhores Medvedev

The Politics of Nuclear Energy

Alan Roberts

The political importance of nuclear power

Modern capitalism has turned increasingly towards technological "advances" that are suspect in the extreme. They are marked by their dubious or plainly negative contribution to human welfare, and by their destructive effects on the environment.

There are some whose harmfulness is now widely recognised — as, for example, the replacement of efficient public transport by a commitment to the private car, the switch to detergents, the massive use of pesticides, the waste of energy in packaging (particularly the non-returnable bottle and the aluminium can).[1]

It is now clear, however, that one particular development — the nuclear power industry — looms above all others, in its ominous implications for the future of humanity, and in its significance as an issue on which mass action against the system's irrationality is likely.

Its predominance derives, firstly, from the sheer magnitude of the economic commitment involved. The leading capitalist countries intend to generate most of their electrical power by nuclear means before the turn of the century, necessitating an unprecedented speed of construction. Over the next decade alone, the US government hopes to see nuclear capacity increased eight-fold; France and Japan aim at roughly fifteen-fold growth. These programmes imply that the USA, for instance, is to spend well over a trillion (million million) dollars on the nuclear industry in the next two and a half decades.[2] It has been estimated that, if the 1985 target is achieved, the nuclear power industry will absorb *over fifty per cent* of gross US capital formation over the next decade.

Next in importance is the transparency of the irrationality involved. It is not a matter of waiting till consequences difficult to foresee have come to pass — as, for example, it was necessary for the polluting effect of detergents actually to show themselves, or for the cities to become congested, polluted and deformed by the automobile. The damage inherent in the nuclear development can be clearly foreseen at this very moment.

The third feature is one of special significance for social change: it concerns the response of the populations in the advanced capitalist countries once they are reached by the arguments against nuclear power. Outstanding here is the example of Sweden, the only country where the issue has been made the subject of more or less formal nation-wide discussion. These discussions, carried on in the course of the year 1974, saw the population swing from approval of the nuclear programme to better than two-to-one opposition. As a result, the government cut its ten-year nuclear target to one-seventh of its former size (from fourteen reactors to two).[3]

Similar responses on a more local scale have been evident in the USA, where the nuclear industry openly expresses its fear that nuclear moratoria (federal or state) will be imposed as a result of public opposition.[4]

Thus it is not simply a question of a valid issue, implying a struggle for all concerned with humanity's future. The campaign against the nuclear commitment also has the character of a transitional demand, striking at the very assumptions of consumerist society, and yet understandable to and acceptable by the people affected.

In countries of the Third World, the political context of the nuclear issue is different but the validity of the struggle is no less clear. It is necessary to emphasise this point particularly, since the proponents of nuclear power often advance arguments allegedly based on the interests of a power-starved Third World — arguments which, as we will see, could hardly be more specious.

Why the nuclear programmes are unacceptable

The dangers associated with nuclear power have been adequately explained in a number of publications, and here we will simply refer the reader to them.[5] They fall under the following main headings:

1. Unscheduled discharges of radiation to the environment, in amounts exceeding the low levels prescribed in normal operation.
2. Catastrophic releases of fuel or waste materials, following on a "melt-down" of the fuel after an accident.

3. Deliberate release (or the threat of it), of radioactive materials, as a measure of terrorism or
   criminal extortion.
4. Environmental damage arising from nuclear
   wastes (whose disposal remains an unsolved
   problem).
5. Undesirable political and social measures adopted
   to cope with these hazards.

The possible magnitude of some of these dangers
can be judged from the simple facts concerning the
highly toxic element plutonium. The maximum
permissible annual intake of plutonium is at present
one millionth of a gram, a quantity known to be
capable of causing cancer (and considered too high
a risk by many authorities, including Britain's
Medical Research Council).[6] But the most com-
mon type of nuclear reactor, in normal operation,
over one year, produces about 200 *kilograms* of
plutonium.

Of course, stringent precautions are taken to
ensure that this and other radioactive poisons are
contained and never reach the atmosphere. But no
system of containment can be perfect, nor verified
with absolute accuracy. (Today, for example, the
inventory of plutonium in a reactor cannot be
checked to better than 1%.)

Suppose then that, by the end of the century,
when upwards of 2,000 reactors are envisaged, a
small fraction of the plutonium generated in a year
"leaks" to the atmosphere — whether by accident
or malevolent design. If the leak is as small as one
hundredth of one per cent of the total, this still
constitutes a maximum permissible dose for every

person in the world, *ten times over.*

The nuclear programme thus embodies a proposal to organise power production around stocks of highly poisonous substances, in quantities almost unimaginably vast in relation to their toxicity. To accept such a programme, one would need to be supremely confident of the social system in which it is to be implemented — confident both of its ability to maintain unprecedentedly high standards of technical skill with absolutely infallible rigour, and of its political and social stability over many generations. The reader can be presumed to lack such confidence.

Despite the quite extraordinary and often ingenious safety routines implemented by the nuclear technologists, whose efforts to achieve the impossible must compel admiration, the safety of the US nuclear industry has already been the target of damaging criticisms. These concern the workings of about fifty reactors in the world's most industrially advanced country; what can be expected when perhaps 2,000 reactors are operating in dozens of countries throughout the world?

Some indication of an answer to this question was given by Jean-Claude Leny, managing director of Francatome. It took the form of a broad hint to investors, that the profitability of nuclear power in France would not be allowed to suffer — like the American industry's — from an exaggerated concern for safety . . . [7]

As for the possibility of malevolent activity, the infant nuclear industry of the USA can already record, amongst other incidents, a threat to crash

a highjacked plane into a reactor, a series of
apparent sabotage attempts in a re-processing plant,
and the selection of nuclear plants for terrorist
blackmail attacks by followers of Charles Manson.[8]

It should be remembered that the possible
damage arising from nuclear catastrophes is not
confined to the existing population in the country
of occurrence.

The very nature of the radioactive threat lends
itself to dispersal in space over national and even
continental boundaries, and to persistence in time
so that generations remote from the present suffer
illness and death (the genetic effects of radiation).
The lesson from the USA in particular is that the
industry's safety standards will tend to be propor-
tional to public concern over the issue; in this light,
the struggle against nuclear power can be seen also
as a simple struggle for human survival on the planet.

The disposal of waste materials from reactors —
and of the worn-out reactors themselves — remains
an unsolved problem. Its magnitude can be gauged
from one figure alone: the annual wastes from an
average reactor today contain 1,000 times the
radioactivity of the Hiroshima bomb. While research
proceeds on possible methods of permanent disposal, the industry contents itself with "waste
management" — that is, retrievable and (it is hoped)
secure methods of storage. Here it should be noted
that the cost of this "temporary" storage (which is
by no means at a satisfactory level of security) will
rise in the next two and a half decades to some
seven billion dollars in the United States alone. It is
easy, then, to understand the fear expressed by US

Environmental Protection Agency experts, of "the possibility that an interim engineered storage system may become permanent solely due to economic costs".[9]

To understand the ominous implications here, one should first note that the interim methods make the poisonous waste "retrievable" — or in other words, accessible. Thus they continually invite malevolently-inspired acquisition or atmospheric release. Also, the time scale of the "permanent" storage required is not in dispute: the long-lasting component of the wastes (particularly plutonium) must be kept rigorously clear of the environment for hundreds of thousands of years — half a million, for safety. This poses the unprecedented problem of finding a storage which will not be disturbed by the *geological* processes that occur over such a time span. Research has not yet proved that such storage exists. Here, once again, an issue of sheer survival is involved, in the struggle to prevent such irresponsibility towards future generations.

The nuclear industry has generally treated critics with disdain, making concessions to them reluctantly and only after public opinion has been roused. But in recent years, some of the more far-sighted proponents of nuclear power have started to recognise the strength of the opposition's case, particularly in the area of "nuclear malevolence". Their proposals for coping with nuclear hazards constitute in themselves an equally ominous political and social threat.

Thus the US Atomic Energy Commission has

proposed a special federal police force devoted to the security of plutonium plants and shipments. It has complained of recent court rulings protecting individual privacy, and requested legislation which would facilitate security checks on nuclear industry personnel.[10]

With the projected growth of the industry, the number of workers affected by such restrictions of civil rights could run into the millions. Already, according to the *New York Times,* Texas state police keep dossiers on opponents of nuclear plants.[11]

The dangers involved here should not be underestimated. A few kilograms of plutonium make an ideal weapon for blackmailing a whole city, since it effectively disperses itself in small particles once exposed to the air. Even graver is the real possibility of constructing a nuclear bomb from plutonium in a reactor's waste, impurities would make it inefficient but, as an experiment has convincingly shown, little skill would be needed to achieve a weapon with the destructive force of about 100 tons of TNT.[12] This would be within the capacity of "amateurs", any government with nuclear power plants would have the facilities to manufacture weapons 100 times more deadly.

After an extortion threat, whether successful or not, an atmosphere of hysteria could well be envisaged, in which authoritarian "law and order" proposals would be difficult to combat. They would even have a certain rationality, inside a globally irrational context.

The many levels of irrationality

The risks just outlined justify the verdict that a major development of nuclear power is irrational, if our criterion is the welfare of humanity. But this is far from the only sense in which we can justly apply the epithet "irrational" to capitalism's nuclear perspectives.

It should first be appreciated that the current nuclear programme is not a long-term solution to the problems of power generation, even in the opinion of capitalism's own analysts. It is projected as merely bridging the gap between the present period marked by rapidly diminishing stocks of oil, and the situation in perhaps three decades or so, when alternative sources of energy will be commercially viable.

The tapping of the sun's energy is one important such alternative, to which capitalism is now belatedly starting to devote increased research and development funds. The primary aim here is to find ways of reducing the capital costs of large-scale solar power plants.

For reasons discussed below, solar power is still seen as less attractive than fusion power — a variety of nuclear plant working on a different principle from the current models. Existing "fission" reactors rely on a controlled version of the nuclear reaction — the "splitting" of a heavy atom such as uranium or plutonium — which in its convulsive release produced the explosion of the Hiroshima bomb. A "fusion" reactor would be based on taming the nuclear reaction underlying the hydrogen bomb, in which light elements "fuse" together to form a heavier element. Steady progress is being made in the research on controlled fusion, particularly since a Soviet breakthrough in this field some years ago — the "Tokamak" development. It is generally believed, however, that several decades will elapse before commercial fusion reactors enter into service, even after a basic design has proved itself in the laboratory.

Thus present nuclear programmes are supposed to justify themselves by their contribution to power needs in the next few decades. But it is precisely in this short term that there arise the most serious doubts of the programme's utility, because of the severe shortage of rich uranium ores.

The industry's major hope here lies in the breeder reactor, whose operating core is wrapped in a "blanket" of natural uranium. Such a reactor will convert the bulk of this uranium into a suitable fuel (normally, less than one per cent of it is available), thus producing (or "breeding") more fuel than it uses up. The world supplies of "burnable" uranium could thus be effectively increased perhaps 70 times over.

Before agreeing with the US administration that breeder reactors thus represent the solution to the nuclear fuel shortage, some facts should be noted. The inherent dangers of the breeder reactor vastly exceed those of the current models, and justify the greater concern and opposition of aware scientists.[15] A whole series of technical difficulties have resulted in repeated postponements of the expected date of operation of a commercial breeder, the latest estimate (probably optimistic) now landing in the 1990s.

'I he significantly higher capital costs, as compared to today's power stations, are likely to result in yet more delays before the buying reluctance of electrical utilities is overcome. And even then, a breeder will take somewhere between 20 and 40 years to produce enough fuel for *one* reactor.

Thus, reliance on the advent of breeders to "stretch" fuel supplies represents a dubious gamble. Yet what the industry is thereby gambling on, is the whole cost-competitiveness of nuclear power.

It is irrationality of another sort which emerges here: the nuclear programme is not even rational on capitalism's own criterion of cost efficiency. Reactors already planned are not assured of a fuel supply which can keep them competitive. Thousands of billions of dollars are to be invested in the hope that something will turn up.

Even with the cheap uranium supply available today, the industry can establish the competitiveness of new plants only by ignoring well-established trends, that would send the price of nuclear-generated electricity skyrocketing. The most important of these trends are, firstly, the staggering escalation in the capital cost of nuclear plants, and secondly, the severe drop in efficiency of nuclear plants after about five years' running.

In May 1975, the Friends of the Earth showed how woefully the relevant utility had under-estimated costs, when they testified against the proposed Rancho Seco 2 reactor near Sacramento (California). Adopting realistic figures for capital cost, interest rates and capacity factor (i.e. efficiency), and for operation, maintenance and decommissioning, the FOE calculation showed that the true cost of a unit of power was nearly *four times* the figure submitted by the utility.[16]

A study of the Grenoble Institute has shown that, in France, nuclear-generated electricity cannot compete with oil at today's prices. In the heating of a household, for example, we can deduce from the study that oil will be cheaper so long as its price remains below $45 a barrel (price in early 1977: approximately $16).[17]

The escalation in capital cost (we consider its explanation later) shows no sign of abating. Of course, that of coal-fired plants also shows an increasing trend, but nothing like as severe — a 1975 study estimated that the *difference* in price between a coal and a nuclear plant was itself increasing by $19 per kilowatt per year.[18] In other words: every year the price of a 1000-megawatt nuclear plant leaps another $19 million above that of its coal-burning rival . . .

The curves of capacity factor against reactor age also show a dismal trend: that the efficiency is low and becoming even lower.[19] All this may make the nuclear commitment seem extraordinary enough; but we have not yet mentioned the most astonishing irrationality of all. Some preliminary remarks are needed.

The power output of a generator of any sort can never represent pure gain, since some power is inevitably consumed in building and running it. In the case of a nuclear reactor, a great deal of power is required merely to set it up in business — to build the station, mine and mill the initial fuel supply, etc. A most important part of this power input occurs at the stage where natural uranium is treated so as to increase the fraction of it which can be "burnt" as fuel — the "enrichment" process.

All this means that the station will be running for some time before it has "paid back" the power used to set it into operation. Calculations of this "break-even" time have been carried out for various reactor designs; they indicate that about two years of normal operation will be needed to repay the power input for construction.

Now consider the effect of a rapid nuclear *programme,* with the number of reactors doubling every few years. To see this effect, let us adopt some definite (though fictitious) figures: suppose a reactor's "pay-back" time is one year (this is unrealistically low), and that the number of reactors is doubling every year (this is unrealistically fast). Suppose also that a reactor takes a year to build (instead of the actual six to nine years).

In year one, no reactors are operating but one is being built; so no power is produced, but one year's output is consumed. In year two, one reactor is operating, but two are under construction, so one year's output is produced, but two are consumed. In year three, three reactors are operating but four are being built; so three years' output is produced, but four are consumed . . .

If the calculation is continued it will be found that the programme uses up more power than it produces, *in every year of its operation.* Of course, in the real world such a programme must come to a halt at some stage, the number of reactors cannot go on doubling each year indefinitely. It is at this point that the nuclear industry will become a net power producer; but until then, it will actually be a net *consumer* of power.

In the real world, also, the figures are not as they are given in the example. But the effect still persists in a modified form, even after we insert the correct data for power input in operation and building time. We still find that the programme will not "break even", in the sense of producing more power than it consumers, for a certain number of years.

Just how many years, will depend on a number of factors: the type of reactor, its operating efficiency, the grade of ore mined, the power consumed in regular operation. But the most detailed calculations available[20] suggest that, inserting the figures appropriate to current programmes, this "break-even" time can easily exceed 20 years.

But this is precisely the period in which the nuclear programme is supposed to compensate for the exhaustion of oil supplies, while the world awaits the arrival of fresh power sources. In other words, the nuclear programme will quite possibly consume more power than it produces, in the very period when it is supposed to be the key factor in power generation!

It should be pointed out that a programme with oil- and coal-burning stations[14] substituted for nuclear, but expanding just as quickly, would make an even worse showing. It is the sheer *speed* of the projected construction programmes which determines their short-term energy inefficiency. But of course, no one plans to build conventional power stations at such a breakneck pace — since no one has the illusion that such a programme would solve any "energy crisis". This illusion attaches only to plans for nuclear power stations, when one "forgets" the energy needed to build them; to puncture the illusion, the sort of energy analysis sketched above is required.

Before arriving at an overall judgement on capitalism's nuclear project, we should appreciate the element of uncertainty which runs through the above analyses. Some of the needed data — what fresh reserves of uranium will be discovered, for instance, or what long-term efficiency (capacity factor) will be achieved by nuclear stations — can only be estimated. Some of the relevant calculations require time and manpower that have not yet been devoted to them, so that only suggestive approximations are available.

However, this very absence of reliable information is itself highly revealing. Let us adopt some of the criteria commonly advanced, *within* a framework of capitalist assumptions, for implementing a new technology, and consider how they are met in the case of nuclear power. Let us see what preconditions should be fulfilled to justify the investment of capital involved.

First, the safety of the new industry should be sufficiently guaranteed, as to obviate the risk of the whole development being aborted at some future date. (This could occur, for example, as a sequel to the catastrophic release of radioactive material, by a plant accident or malevolent design.

The public reaction could well make it politically impossible to continue operation of the existing plants, and force the abandonment of the large amounts of capital they represented.)

Secondly, the programmes adopted should actually achieve their declared goals: that is, to produce significantly more power than they consume, in the vital period of the next few decades.

Thirdly, the electricity produced should be competitive in cost with that generated by "conventional" (oil- or coal-fired) stations.

Fourtly, plants should not be projected unless they are guaranteed a suitable supply of fuel over their working lifetime.

Fifthly, the financial mechanisms should exist that will enable the "consumer" (i.e. the electrical utilities) to obtain the capital needed to buy the reactors concerned.

It is when we review these reasonable criteria that there emerges the full irrationality of capitalism's nuclear plans: it has not been demonstrated that they satisfy a *single one* of these basic requirements.

At best, the nuclear industrialists can be regarded as undertaking a colossal gamble. They are gambling that no catastrophic accident will occur in the short term, despite the narrow squeaks already in the record. They are gambling that fresh high-grade ore reserves, or a technically and commercially viable breeder reactor, will be available in time. They are gambling that the trend to ever-higher capital costs, and the decline with age in the efficiency of the functioning reactors, will be reversed, or economically compensated for by increased cost of conventional fuels.

In the USA, they are even gambling that "something will turn up" in the way of finance, to permit the purchase of reactors by the electrical utilities. (Early in 1975, some 60% of reactor orders in the USA had been cancelled or postponed, mainly because of the refusal of finance houses to lend the purchase money.)[21]

It is true that capitalist enterprises have been known to "gamble" before this — to spend on research and development, or to launch on the production of a new commodity whose market was not assured. But we remind the reader of the sums involved in this particular gamble — well over a thousand billion dollars in the remainder of this century, in the United States alone.

It would be easy to conclude that the gods of history, with the destruction of capitalism high on their agenda, are staging their proverbial prologue of induced lunacy. But a pat verdict of "guilty but insane", even if supported by the evidence, hardly goes far enough; it is also necessary to *understand*.

The attempt to reach even a partial understanding is mandatory, and not only because of the importance of the nuclear programme in itself, both economically and politically. There is another issue involved: that of the dynamic of the capitalist economy in the present period. It may be that the nuclear industry can serve as a paradigm, showing — in not-so-small miniature — the emergence of new trends or changes in the relative weight of ones already known.

The Energy Company's Gamble

There are few industries, even today, as heavily
monopolised as the nuclear industry. When one
says "pressurised-water reactor", one says Westinghouse; and "boiling-water reactor" likewise means
General Electric. And these two types, built by
the two giants directly or through subsidiaries and
licensing agents throughout the capitalist world,
account for over 85% of the nuclear-component
industry.

The powerful pressure of these multi-national
corporations exerts itself even on those countries
possessing their own proven reactor designs. Thus
Francis Perrin, formerly the French high commis-
sioner for atomic energy, has recently complained
of the "monolithism" of the French nuclear programme (even while rubbishing the anti-nuclear
campaign as "based only on totally false assertions"
and on declarations "devoid of all objective value").
He recalls General de Gaulle's decision (December
12, 1967) to proceed with the construction of two
large reactors of a French design (graphite-moder-
ated, gas-cooled, fuelled by natural uranium) that
has elsewhere proved itself. The blocking of this
decision he lays to the account only of some un-
named highly-placed civil servants, also responsible
for the present plan to instal "almost exclusively"
the pressurised-water reactors of . . . Westinghouse.

He calls, but without much apparent faith in the
likelihood of success, for the French programme to
include more "diversification", a feature not sufficiently provided by the present inclusion of some
boiling-water reactors from . . . General Electric.[22]

The weight of the multi-nationals has been felt even in Britain, the country whose own design of gas-cooled reactor pioneered the commercial generation of nuclear electricity. Hot debate raged after the Central Electricity Generating Board and the National Nuclear Corporation both recommended a switch to the American light-water reactor. But under intensive questioning before a House of Commons Select Committee, they were unable to justify their recommendations, and the Government decided not to switch — for the time being, at least.

The revelations from Lockheed and other firms have made notorious one of the processes by which the multi-nationals "conquer" foreign markets: old-fashioned bribery of influential natives. It should not be assumed, however, that this is always the predominant factor. Sheer size counts for a great deal — as illustrated in the unhappy case of the design of an international computing language. The world's experts agreed on a suitable language, and devoted much effort to its elaboration. But their eugenic offspring, Algol runs a very poor second in its breadth of social acceptance to the inferior language, Fortran — which was born with a silver spoon in its mouth, sired by the market-dominating IBM .

In another direction, a still vaster oligopolistic structure is shaping up, as the leading oil companies complete their transformation into what has been accurately described as "energy companies". Already in 1971, the oil giants were responsible for the milling of some 40% of US

uranium; their coal production amounted to 20%
of the US total, and their acquisition of coal
reserves guaranteed their future dominance in
the industry (one oil company alone — Humble —
was the nation's second largest coal owner). In
the nuclear field, Gulf Oil (with the third largest
assets — about $9 billion — of any oil company)
had set up Gulf General Atomic.[23]

This latter company threatens Britain's lead in
gas-cooled reactors, and already in 1972 there was
"consternation in the nuclear industry" as a con-
sequence, according to one writer.[24] Gulf promises
delivery of high-temperature gas reactors (an
advanced design) around 1980.

But if this represents competition with the
dominant light-water American reactors, is similar
consternation apparent among the ruling giants?
Hardly; the chairman of Gulf General Atomic,
E. Prockett, happens to sit on the board of Westinghouse also.

A thrust towards monopolisation is built into
the nuclear project. A single plant of today's typical
size — a thousand megawatts of electrical power —
costs upwards of half a billion dollars, and smaller
units are neither readily available nor called for in
quantity. Companies with assets not running into
the billions can hardly hope for a sizeable share of
such a market, nor risk the investments needed to
establish themselves.

The dynamic of capitalism's nuclear project has
been spelled out — with some naive admiration —
by Simon Rippon, the editor of a technical journal
noted for its fervent, not to say fanatical, nuclear
partisanship.

". . . The big industrial concerns have not entered the
business for quick profits — indeed, most of the companies that have entered the nuclear business around the
world have been shaken to their foundations by losses
on early projects and few can see dramatic profits in the
future. For the most part the position of industry is that
the long term direction of energy supply is going to be
increasingly in the direction of nuclear power and therefore for the well-being of their company they must establish a foothold in this sector of the business in spite of
the heavy initial costs."[25]

It may be doubted whether the "foothold" is
being seized as reluctantly as Rippon makes it
sound. For the larger giants, nuclear power spells
centralisation, size, growth. The prospect before
them is an intoxicating one: the power industry
swollen to a size unheard of, its relative weight in
the economy enhanced several times over, and all
of it within the grasp of one or two amicably-
coexisting combines .

The power industry as a whole can of course
anticipate such an increase in its relative share of
the gross national product, since the power needs
of industrial capitalist society grow faster than the
GNP itself. In Japan, for instance, official projec-
tions are for a growth of 4% in the GNP, compared
to 6.2% for the electrical output.[26] Using this data,
a simple calculation shows that the proportion of
the GNP represented by electricity output (i.e., its
relative weight in the economy) will be double
what it is now, in a little over 30 years.

It is only this perspective which can explain the
gambles they are taking, and pressuring govern-
ments to take. They are not really gambling that

no catastrophes will occur, that no hitches will hold up the breeder reactor when it is needed, that the nuclear project will remain cost-competitive.

What they are really gambling on — and from their viewpoint, it is a "rational" risk to take — is that their economic and especially their political weight in society will be so massive, that society has no option but to make their bets come home.

It is the next decade which is crucial for this outcome. By 1985, the nuclear share in electricity production is designed to reach, in the leading capitalist countries, the 10% level or close to it (the USA, 13%; the EEC, 17%; France, 30%).

Within the present structure of industrial capitalism, it is hard to envisage a situation in which such proportions of the power supply could simply be switched off, no matter how powerful the arguments in terms of human welfare or even of economic efficiency.

Perhaps a catastrophic "melt-down", releasing millions of curies of radioactivity, killing tens of thousands of people, damaging property to the extent of billions of dollars? Studies by the American Atomic Energy Commission have shown that accidents could well have such a scope.[27] But if society really depends on the nuclear branch of its power industry in order to continue along its accustomed path, and if this path can still claim an overall acceptance, then an alternative to a shutdown would be the adoption of "firm measures", allegedly ensuring that such disasters could not recur.

Such measures, whose shape was sketched in the

AEC report mentioned earlier, would be repressive and authoritarian in the extreme; and there can be little doubt that among the movements heavily repressed would be any spreading panic or mobilising action in connection with nuclear power.

But if nuclear power reveals itself as unarguably wasteful? Suppose the tendencies for nuclear plants to decline in efficiency with age, and to require more and more capital for their construction, become so pronounced that, on economic grounds, they should simply be replaced by non-nuclear methods of power generation. Would not this be a situation disastrous to the nuclear industry, one in which their gamble had definitively failed?

Possibly — if they allowed such a situation to arise. But, as a Harvard-MIT study pointed out in the *Technology Review*:

> "The price of usable energy from oil, coal or uranium now has little to do with the marginal production cost of any of these resources . . . Instead, the price of energy from alternative technologies is the result of a complicated process of assigning relative values to a variety of energy-producing resources and technologies by those who either control or require these resources and technologies. This process is both intensely and inherently political."[18]

In assessing the degree of control over energy prices, it is vital to realize that we are not dealing with an isolated handful of reactor manufacturers — more and more, the Energy Company becomes a powerful reality, and the relative pricing of the various methods of electricity generation falls increasingly under its control. "Free competition" between the various primary fuels started to lose its reality many years ago, as the oil companies moved over into the mining of coal, of uranium, into the processing of uraniums and — through subsidiaries and affiliates — into the building of reactors. Their influence will be exerted to fix prices that reflect, not the resultant of competitive forces, and not the realities of cost of effectiveness but simply the interests of their own needs for expansion, investment and profit.

Thus, if the nuclear industry is gambling, it knows in advance that the dice will be loaded in its favour. And even if its luck turns unexpectedly bad, and the table runs against it incessantly, there remains a further and decisive recourse: it can have a word with the management . . .

Consumerist capitalism needs the power industry; it even needs its continuous and sizeable expansion. The State which administers that system never runs on the basis of one-capitalist-one-vote, or even one-million-dollars-one-vote; always some animals in that particular jungle play the role of the king of beasts. The Energy Company, more than half nuclearised by the turn of the century, will certainly supply a king or two, perhaps even a king of kings. Such personages do not need to fear bankruptcy, or even a missed dividend. If even the smaller predators like Lockheed, Boeing or Gruman can depend on sympathetic intervention by the State in their hour of need, what will be beyond the power of the Energy Company?

Indeed, nuclear power has already benefited crucially from State support, and not only in the billions lavished on research and development, whose results the corporations simply take over. Another important parcel of "aid" has been delivered by the US government plants enriching uranium. The Westinghouse and GE reactors require fuel that has passed through this expensive process, and their success in penetrating the market is due in no small measure to the artifically-low price assured by what amounts to a concealed State subsidy; an advantage which has not gone unnoticed by their competitors:

> "Ned Franklin, chairman and managing director of Britain's Nuclear Power Company . . . maintains that the price of uranium enrichment is now fixed by essentially political considerations. Enrichment is dominated by the US, which supplies most of the enrichment requirements of the western world. According to people working in the US's nuclear industry, the prevailing price of enrichment is about half what it would be if the industry had to build new facilities and operate them at a profit.
>
> "The problem is that enrichment is subsidised by the use of old plant that was paid for as part of the weapons programme; enrichment plants are supplied with subsidised electricity; and there is no charge for research and development."[28]

With such marks of favour already acquired, there seems little that the Energy Company needs to fear — unless, of course, it confronts an enemy whom even the State must treat with caution.

Creating the "objective facts"

The socialist movement has suffered for many generations from the illusion that technology is value-free. Adopting a misleading schema in which an essentially non-political "base" (the forces of production) is to be simply taken over and endowed with a different "superstructure" (socialist relations of production), it has failed to appreciate the political content of that technological base.

Even Lenin is on record as succumbing to this error, when he went so far as to laud the Taylor system (time and motion study) and urge its adoption in the Soviet Union. It should be noted that a question mark must now be put over the "technological rationality" of the assembly-line method itself; can it really be justified even on the narrow criterion of "stepping up production"? This most alienating of all technological practices needs re-examination in the light of recent industrial experiments (particularly in Sweden) based on a self-managed working team, rather than a single worker permanently assigned to one stultifying operation on the line.

That technology, and the line of development of technology, are alike political, is nowhere more evident today than in capitalism's nuclear project. It is illuminating to consider the non-nuclear alternatives for power supply, their undesirability from monopoly capital's viewpoint, and the way that an apparently inevitable technological progress along nuclear lines is actually the result of highly political decisions.

A source of nuclear power has supplied mankind with the overwhelming bulk of its energy throughout history; it is the sun, a giant reactor successfully employing the fusion process without pollution and without wasting non-renewable fuel reserves (over a time scale of several billions of years, at any rate). Serious studies of the world's energy problems almost invariably urge the priority of research and development in the field of solar power as the most attractive prospect for mankind.

But it might be asked: how real is this prospect of solar power? What are the technological data on its practicability as a large-scale resource? How does its level of development compare with other energy sources, and what is its promise in the short term?

Questions such as these are posed at the wrong level; they seek as answers a recital of "bare" technological data, not themselves embodying politico-economic decisions, but supplying the value-free facts on which such decisions can be based. It is true that there are circumstances (very restricted, and usually of little social interest) in which such a dichotomy of fact and value has a relative validity; but the present questions are not located in a context even remotely appropriate to such a division.

Large-scale nuclear reactors actually exist; nuclear power moved out of the laboratory many decades ago, into the province of the architect and the engineer. Large-scale solar plants, on the contrary, remain in the anteroom of research and development. Is this a "bare" technological fact? Only in the most abstract sense; in the real world, the genesis, understanding and future implications of this "fact" must be sought in the sphere of political economy.

For there is no autonomous, independently-evolving sphere of "technological progress" which thus made nuclear plants arrive before solar. Nuclear technology was developed in response to conscious decisions on the allocation of manpower and funds — inspired originally by the search for more destructive weapons, and later by the attractiveness for monopoly capitalism of the peculiar qualities of nuclear power.

The failure to allocate corresponding resources to solar power research was the complementary decision that helped to create the "technological facts" as they now exist. And of course, similar remarks can be made about projects to tap the earth's subterranean heat (geothermal power), or to utilize the tides.

Thus the facts are purely technological only in abstraction, inside a conceptual schema that isolates from its social context an abstract history of "technological progress". In the concrete world of things as they have been and as they are, these facts are born already "dressed" in a political-economic penumbra that accompanies them always, determines their significance and points to their future possibilities.

This can be seen very clearly, when we consider the prospects of solar power vis-à-vis nuclear, over the next couple of decades. The "facts" involved here are being created right now, and a glance at US budgetary allocations will show us what facts the Energy Company hopes to bring about: for every dollar spent this year on solar research, more than eight dollars will be spent on one nuclear project alone — the breeder reactor.[29]

It is not hard to understand why monopoly

capital is so lukewarm towards solar power. The latter lends itself admirably to decentralisation, small installations, a minimum investment of capital; these are fatal flaws from the viewpoint of the giant corporation. The "technical" advantages — inexhaustible energy supply, absence of pollution, longevity of the installation, low maintenance expenses — cannot compensate for these inbuilt deficiencies . . . It has been well said, that solar power would fare very differently if only General Electric could buy the sun!

The sad fact is, however, that solar leases are not yet open to takeover bids; and so the corporations are doing the next best thing: planning to build their own sun . . . For there *is* some corporation interest in solar power, provided the inbuilt vices just mentioned can be eliminated, and the project made capital-intensive, large-scale, highly centralised. These are precisely the qualities of the Satellite Solar Power Station, emanating from Arthur D. Little Inc., Grumman, Raytheon and Textron. A giant satellite a kilometre across will absorb sunlight, convert it to microwave radiation and beam it down to a seven-kilometre receiver on the Earth's surface, generating from three to 15 times the output of a single large nuclear plant.[30]

In principle, the solar power source can be a highly flexible device, adaptable in size to meet a wide range of demand and providing access to power for the most isolated community. A minimum of capital investment can provide a self-sufficient source for an indefinite period, and one uniquely compatible with ecological requirements.

These features can hardly be recognized in the satellite project, which achieves the near-impossible: a solar power source demanding on enormous capital investment, suitable for insertion into only the very largest national electricity grids, taking no advantage of solar radiation's great suitability for direct heating of homes and workplaces, and delivering, with its giant receiving antennae, an insult to the environment on a new and monstrous scale.

We do monopoly capital an injustice, then, if we evaluate its nuclear programme as nothing more than a technological project. Quite apart from its inherent hazards to humanity, its adoption would then become incomprehensible in view of the serious doubts as to nett energy production, security of investment, reliability of fuel supply and cost-competitiveness.

But actually it must be seen as a project in a much wider sense: namely, as a *social* project, predicated upon a definite social structure and aiming to develop that structure in a definite direction.

The social structure concerned is that of capitalism in its consumerist phase, where a widening gap — between a potential for self-managing fulfilment, and a reality of hierarchical repression — is papered over with a policy of consumerist concessions. Destruction of the environment is implicit in such a society; this connection has been analysed in some detail elsewhere, and will not be further discussed here.[31]

The power needs of such a society are vast and

ever increasing, and it indeed faces a 'crisis" in the prospect of exhaustion of oil reserves, combined with a severe pollution problem from coal-burning power sources. But, for reasons which will be clear from the discussion above, the giant corporations which dominate its technical development can hardly be enthusiastic about the rational lines of solution advocated even by its own experts: elimination of wasteful energy consumption, reduction in the growth of the electrical power industry, development of alternative sources such as solar, geothermal and tidal power.

It is true that nuclear power, too, has its disadvantages — it may, for example, weaken the fabric of social control by the destructive or blackmailing opportunities it creates for dissident groups. But in lending itself to centralisation, expansion, and domination by a few industrial giants, it accords well with the dynamic of consumerist capitalism — which would be hard put to accommodate policies of energy conservation and the strangling of growth.

Of course, the system will have to adjust itself to the pecularities of this new power source. The Energy Company may have to distort market and pricing mechanisms more grotesquely still, to nudge along the consumption of nuclear-generated electricity and the purchase of nuclear reactors. Massive and direct State intervention may be required to ensure the industry's future, with the perhaps grudging consent, or even against the opposition, of industrialists in other sectors. And measures of social discipline will almost certainly be called for,

restricting civil rights and limiting the activities of
protest movements, to provide the safeguards
needed once society depends for its life-blood —
electrical power — on one or two thousand in-
credibly poisonous sources. Such expectations may
well appear repugnant, but they cannot be dubbed
fantastic; they are solidly based on existing values
and assumptions, those which demand the constant
expansion of the commodity market and, to an
even greater extent, of electricity output.

But these values and assumptions do not go
unchallenged, and there is nothing fatalistically
inevitable about the scenario sketched above. We
have been looking at the political economy of
capitalism today; but a different political economy
is also shaping itself, already in conflict with its
older rival and by no means invariably vanquished.
We must now look at the forces behind this alternative view, take note of their accomplishments up
to the present and estimate their possibilities in the
future.

The Political Economy of Contestation

Opposition to the construction of nuclear power
plants has developed, over the last five years, into a
world-wide campaign of significant scope and
impact. Despite the power of the corporative forces
committed to the nuclear programme, the journals
of the nuclear industry overtly and repeatedly
express the fears roused in them by the achieve-
ments and potential of their opponents.

"Things can't get worse or can they?' was the
gloomy title of an editorial in *Nuclear News* (April
1975), which went on:

"The likelihood of a nuclear moratorium, either national or in one or more states, is difficult to assess. Judged from the discussion of it among observers of the Washington DC scene, and from the amount of activity on the state level, the situation is not encouraging for the light-water reactor industry, and is much worse for the breeder reactor."

A writer in *Nuclear Engineering International* (July 1974, p.579) raised a similar possibility: "However unjustified, public opposition to nuclear energy may rise to such levels that forecast installation programmes have to be scrapped . . . ".

Superficially, some of the nuclear industry's major troubles seem unconnected with the anti-nuclear opposition. We have seen how, in early 1975, about 60 per cent of the nuclear plants on order had been deferred or cancelled — a severe blow to the Administration's nuclear plans forming part of "Project Independence". This setback is usually attributed to the "cash squeeze'" of the time, which made Wall Street reluctant to lend the electrical utilities the capital with which to purchase reactors.

It is true that some orders for "conventional" power stations were likewise affected; but even so, the finance houses do not seem too enthusiastic about the economic future of nuclear-generated electricity. Nor are they alone in their doubts.

Robert F. Gilkeson, chairman of the Edison Electric Institute, was reported as saying at the April 1975 American Power Conference that "it is impossible in present circumstances to build a power plant that will yield a satisfactory return on investment."[32] After analysing the poor performance of the older reactors, David Comey doubts if the banking community will be willing to finance the nuclear programme, and suggests that General Electric, Westinghouse and other nuclear firms may "join Lockheed, Boeing and Grumman on the rolls of corporations bailed out of costly technological misadventure by the taxpayers."

It might seem that here, at any rate, we have unearthed some "bare" technological facts which, despite all their contortions and figure-juggling, the nuclear corporations cannot conceal. Nuclear power is just too costly, and that's that . . . Or is it? Let us investigate a little more deeply:

Nuclear power stations are usually situated well away from the densely populated areas in which the electricity is actually consumed. This entails a two-fold economic penalty, as Hohenemser points out:

First, that part of the energy released which is not converted into electricity becomes pure waste, since the consumers are not sufficiently near to allow this energy to be used for residential and commercial heating and cooling. Thus the very promising concept of a "total energy system" cannot be realised, and the surplus energy becomes waste heat whose disposal is a problem. But the energy thus wasted is more than double the electrical energy utilized .

Secondly, the additional distance over which electricity must be transmitted means additional investment in transmission lines, and additional losses in energy.

Furthermore, conservative operating procedures are adopted to prevent possible accidents; operating costs rise because of the need to protect workers from radiation. As Hohenemser sums it up: "The accident risk, though small, leads to large economic penalties."

It will be apparent that these economic penalties cannot be regarded as solely economic in origin. The pressures which force the nuclear station to be sited remotely, or to adopt stringent and costly precautions, depend intimately on the level of popular suspicion of nuclear power, and of legal-political activity based upon that suspicion.

Thus it is difficult to interpret these economic difficulties of nuclear power as pure "technological data". But further analysis makes the point emerge even more sharply:

Perhaps the most important single factor telling against the economic future of nuclear power is the continuing escalation in capital cost of the nuclear plants, as compared to coal-burning plants. The reasons for this escalation have been carefully analysed in *Technology Review* (February 1975) by Bupp (Harvard) and Derian, Donsimoni and Treitel (MIT).

They find that total cost is strongly correlated with the length of the licensing period — i.e. the time elapsed before the plant is licensed by the Atomic Energy Commission (AEC) to enter into operation. Under US law, citizens can "intervene", on safety, environmental and other grounds, to oppose the granting of the licence or secure its postponement.

It is this intervention process, they show, which carries the responsibility for prolongation of the licensing period and the correlated rise in capital costs:

> "The American administrative and judicial processes afford . . . critics ample opportunity to impede the rate of reactor commercialisation. The principal consequence has been dramatic cost increases. The extreme critics of nuclear power have been at least partially successful in their efforts to force a downward re-evaluation of the social value of reactor technology.
>
> ". . . The issue here is not merely technical or economical, but is inherently political: Present trends in nuclear reactor costs can be interpreted as the economic result of a fundamental debate on nuclear power within the US community. Beyond its economic effects, the real issue of this debate is the social acceptability of nuclear power . . ."

(It should perhaps be recalled that critics of nuclear power are not free to hold up construction at will; they must show that the particular project fails to satisfy environmental requirements, existing radiation-release standards, AEC regulations . . . And it is precisely this kind of deficiency that they have been able to establish, time and again.)

Perhaps the second most ominous trend, for nuclear-power competitiveness, is that of declining capacity factor (efficiency) as plants grow older. A detailed study of the reasons for this decline is still in progress, but some contributing factors are already apparent, which are associated with the radioactive dangers in a nuclear plant and the public consciousness of them. For instance, the discovery in September 1974 of cracks in the cooling pipes of a US reactor resulted in the shutting-down (for inspection) of all reactors of the same type; this would hardly have been done in the case of conventional power stations. Nor would it have been done, in all probability, if the public were less inclined to associate danger with the word "nuclear".

Unprecedented maintenance difficulties can arise in nuclear reactors; the simple welding of a crack becomes a large-scale operation in which hundreds of workers have to be deployed, when the crack occurs in a region of such high radioactivity that each worker can remain there for no longer than a few minutes . . . Here again, the long campaign which forced the AEC to tighten up its radiation standards, and the heightened public awareness which resulted, should not be overlooked as a relevant factor.

We see, then, that the Energy Company has not got the field to itself; there are other political choices and actions which are significantly affecting the "bare economic facts" of nuclear power production. And of course, their effect on the political decisions in this field is even more noticeable — as shown, for example, by the severe reduction in the Swedish nuclear programme for the next decade (from 14 reactors to two) already mentioned above.

We will not go on to list the successes of the anti-nuclear campaign in such other countries as Japan; the above is enough to show that significant effects can be achieved. This is all the more remarkable, being given that most of the radical left, in most of these struggles, have followed a policy of more-or-less benevolent abstention .

It should be said, in conclusion, that the anti-nuclear movement is likely to find its path much thornier in the future. The year 1975 must be recorded as the year of the great backlash, when the nuclear industry geared itself up on an international scale to launch a well-organised counter-offensive.

In Washington, a pro-nuclear rally was scheduled for the middle of May — "The first time that the industry, which has traditionally avoided direct action on its own behalf, has set out to make itself heard", according to a supporter. This rally was to unite representatives of the Atomic Industrial Forum, the non-profit utilities, the National Association of Electric Companies (investor-owned utilities) and the national rural electrical co-operative association.[33]

In April, the European Nuclear Society met in Paris, at a conference reported as though it were a similar propagandist rally.[34] Westinghouse assigned a team of propagandists in Pittsburgh to the job of "rebutting" environmentalist objections to nuclear power stations.[35] The Atomic Energy Commission in Australia — a country with no commercial reactors — ran an internal study course for its staff, slanted towards the justification of nuclear power. (The export of uranium is a current issue in Australia.)

In launching this propaganda offensive on a global scale, the corporations tacitly acknowledge both the importance of the nuclear development for the immediate future of consumerist capitalism, and their appreciation of the strength of mass suspicion in its regard. It is vital that the left show an equal appreciation of these factors, participating wholeheartedly in the anti-nuclear campaign and strengthening its connection with the overall struggle against an irrational social system.

The left is hampered in fulfilling this role by the misleading theory (among others discussed further on) that the technological sphere evolves autonomously, independent of political action. The philosophical defects in this view have been surveyed above; after considering the particular case of the nuclear power industry, we can see how woefully it fails to explain the facts and the dynamic of this major component of capitalist planning in the decades to come.

Of course, the traditional marxist view never entirely overlooked this phenomenon; but it was usually content with a mere mention of the existence of "reciprocal interaction", or of the "mutual independence" of the various sectors of the social "totality". The analysis itself usually proceeded in a strictly one-way direction, with the political exercising little if any direct influence on the technological or economic.

It would be wrong to claim that this method has now lost all validity; but it is apparent that, in the case of nuclear power, it does not give even a good first approximation to the truth. It is difficult to conceive of this holding good only for one special and exceptional case, when that case looms so large in terms of economic significance and investment allocation. Are we not rather looking at a paradigm of capitalism's development in this present phase, with deep lessons for the left and its programme of radical reconstruction?

Whatever the misconceptions of some of its practitioners, marxism could never have been properly interpreted as a variety of economic determinism, in which technological development exerted a one-way influence on the remaining structures of society. Marxism separated itself decisively from such theories by its standpoint of class analysis, so that the technological sphere can be effective only when mediated through the prevailing class interests.

The interests of the capitalist class are not to be conceived as simply the making of a fast buck. They include also the preservation of a structure of industry which will enable the capitalist system to continue; and it is precisely this continuance of the centralised, large-scale, ever-expanding economy, based on a market of "created demand", which the environmental crises today put in serious doubt.

In this situation, the larger investment decisions must be seen as political decisions, in which the longer-term interests of the system must take precedence over narrowly-conceived "economic" interests. But as political acts, they become vulnerable to the attacks of political opponents — a vulnerability which the outstandingly irrational nuclear industry knows only too well, as it nurses its wounds and lashes back .

Thus, in intervening in struggles over the shape of the economy the left should not be hampered by any lingering compunctions, perhaps based on recollections of the "Luddite" period, of the "utopian machine-wreckers" (recollections which are revealed as obsolete by the facts above, and which were generally inaccurate historically in any case). Otherwise, they will be leaving unchallenged some of the most significant political decisions of the giant corporations, carrying immediate threats to the world of today and even sowing the seeds of disaster for humanity's whole future.

A Digression: the USSR and the "Third World"

The analysis above is focused on the advanced capitalist countries, and should not be extrapolated beyond them. The other major sectors of the world merit a separate if briefer discussion.

With a total list of only 25 plants, including those under construction or on order, the nuclear programme of the USSR is insignificant in comparison to that of the USA, which is some 15 times greater in power output. Indeed, France's alone outstrips the Soviet's in capacity (by about 50 per cent).[36]

This lesser level of development is not to be explained by an initial technological lag — the first Soviet nuclear station opened in 1958, ahead of every other country in the world save one (Britain).

Nor does it stem from any ideological aversion to nuclear power. Official Soviet doctrine sees no problem in the inherent centralized nature of nuclear power; no problem in the superhuman standards demanded for safe operation in the long term: no problem in the disposal of radioactive wastes.

Indeed, the absence of genuine public discussion on the issues involved in nuclear power has allowed the Soviet nuclear industry to "solve" its disposal problems with a breathtaking lightmindedness: high-level radioactive wastes are simply pumped under pressure into deep permeable zones. Thus they are irretrievable; in insecure liquid form; and moreover (because of the high pressure of the injection), a threat to the stability of the whole region; disposal methods with these objectionable features would never be permitted in the USA or Europe.[37]

In explaining the Soviet tardiness in nuclear development, one cannot overlook the abundance of its coal, oil and hydropower resources. But the absence of private ownership also seems relevant here, saving the USSR from some of the more spectacularly irrational features of capitalism's technological policies. At least its power supply will not be shaped by the imperial adventures of an Energy Company.

The situation of nuclear power in the Third World is of direct relevance to the controversy in the industrially advanced capitalist countries. For defenders of nuclear power there often rest their case on the needs of Third World countries; short of coal, faced with rising oil prices, and yet starved of energy for their economic take-off, their only hope, allegedly, is the power of the atom.

This argument is either cynical or simply ignorant. A United Nations analysis has revealed the true situation, referring first to the Third World's

> ". . . very poor infrastructure of technology and non-availability of trained manpower to handle the reactors and other nuclear plants. The probability of nuclear accidents and consequently of dangers to human environment are bound to be far greater in these countries. Further it is doubtful whether these countries could afford to spend an additional $3-4 billion towards the foreign exchange cost of nuclear facilities during the next 25 years which will be the years of financial stress in these countries arising from pressure of population and scarcity of food. Moreover, the small size of the national electric power grids can integrate only small nuclear power plants which are at present not being manufactured . . . "[38]

This last point is at present vital: the leading corporations are simply not interested in building reactors small enough to fit Third World needs. And they appear to remain adamant despite pleas by nuclear protagonists in the specialist literature, and even by leading figures at the September 1974 conference of the International Atomic Energy Authority.[39]

Evidently they prefer to fight one battle at a time. Once the developed "heartland" has been conquered for nuclear power, it may be time to think of the outskirts.

The people of the Third World have no interest in speeding up the process of their "nuclearisation"; the UN comments above show this clearly enough. Financially, the higher capital cost of nuclear plants would deepen their dependence on the imperialist countries, who are skilled in exacting a political price for "development loans". Technologically, an important part of their industry would be in the hands of metropolitan experts for several decades. Economically, even a medium-sized plant would

usually constitute by itself a high degree of concentration of power supply, and favour a centralisation
of industry and a grandiosity of construction
squarely opposed to the real needs of the bulk of
the population. (When the majority of the population have no access to a power point, the arrival of
a nuclear plant can hardly do otherwise than distort
the economy further. What benefits have flowed
through to the mass of people in those underdeve-
loped countries already boasting nuclear stations —
Pakistan, India, Spain?)

The Role of the Left

In the campaign against nuclear power — as in most
of the campaigns on environmental issues — it has
been exceptional to find the political vanguards
actually in the van. Those with a pro-Moscow
orientation have usually endorsed nuclear power as
wholeheartedly and irresponsibly as the Soviet
bureaucracy itself. Others have remained on the
sidelines, or grudgingly joined in at the rear, because
of ideological suspicions about the movement's
purity in general, and its compatibility with their
programme in particular.

In its most extreme form, this suspicion leads to
a dismissal of the anti-nuclear struggle — indeed of
environmentalist issues in general — as a trendy
middle-class phenomenon that does not interest
the working class, and hence is no concern of the
true revolutionary, who will concentrate on the
real issues: those at the point of production and in
the realm of State power.

Such a class characterisation of the environmentalist movement has greater difficulty reconciling itself with the facts now, than it might have had a few years ago; a weakness more serious still, is the implied judgement of an issue, not on its merits as a valid transitional demand, but on its present level of working-class penetration.

It might be worth pointing out how neatly this attitude reverses the approach to social problems that was typical of Karl Marx. Absorbed above all else by humanity's need for the overthrow of capitalism, Marx had an eagle eye — whether as journalist or as theoretician — for movements which contained the seed of revolution. Seeing the revolutionary potential of the working class, he thereafter focused his theoretical and practical activity on the needs and development of the working class movement.

The attitude we are examining turns this upside down. An attachment to the role of the working class — or rather, to a particular selection from Marx's writings about it in his day — serves it as a reason for ignoring what was Marx's first concern: evidence of revolutionary potential in any movements or strata in the contemporary world. If such schools of thought turn a blind eye to the environmental movement, their vision is not much keener when it comes to the liberation movements of women, blacks or gays. Eventually, after the passage of time, some Galileo may be able to persuade them to look through his telescope. But they will need first to be convinced that the sights they will see can somehow (perhaps tortuously) be reconciled with the true reality — which for them (as it never was for Marx) is constituted by their *doctrine*.

A widespread climate of such opinions can exert a damaging influence — as it appears to have done even to a talented and perceptive analyst such as Hans-Magnus Enzenberger.

His article, "A Critique of Political Ecology", dissects and exposes some of the best-publicised "doomsday ecologists", such as Ehrlich, in a study of considerable value. But the reader will search in vain for any recommendation that the left should participate in, and endeavour to guide, mass movements to defend the environment — from nuclear contamination or anything else.[40]

Despite Enzenberger's clear recognition of the possibility of what he calls "ecological rebellions" and "uncontrollable riots", he is uneasy about the "dangers" of participation by the left, and can only recommend that "a long process of clarification will be necessary . . . "

By confining itself to the study and to a role of instruction from afar, the left will indeed avoid the risk of being "used" — just as an army is in no danger of being tricked and outmanoeuvred if it keeps clear of the battlefield. But, specialising from environmental issues in general to the nuclear question in particular, it must be asked whether the ground should really be surrendered to the enemy so easily.

The historical import of the nuclear power programme derives from the current plight of modern capitalism: based firmly on consumerist values and concessions, it sees the development of that consumerism heading inexorably towards the destruction of the environment. The coming exhaustion of oil reserves is one harbinger of the crisis, and has prompted a reckless acceleration of the nuclear programmes, in an attempt to ensure, at whatever cost, that consumerist capitalism will have available the centralised sources of power it needs.

The struggle over nuclear power thus poses questions about the very shape of society itself — as any intervention in this struggle quickly reveals. For it is impossible to adopt a purely negative stance, attacking nuclear power but proposing no alternative energy policy.

Many of the reformist critics understand this well, and offer programmes which envisage the attainment of social energy goals without the use of nuclear power, but which usually involve sizeable reductions in energy consumption by various methods of conservation.

But such a conservation policy would represent an extraordinary historical "turn" by a consumerist capitalist society, wedded as it is to continual expansion; a society, moreover, in which the relative weight of the "Energy Company" grows day by day. Can such a society significantly restrict its energy consumption over a whole business cycle -- for example, in a time of recession, will it throttle down on vitally needed expansion plans, simply because they are energy-expensive? And what would be the social and political reverberations of such energy-conserving policies as were adopted?

These important questions usually get scant consideration from moderate advocates of conservation. In contrast, those already convinced of the need for radical social change are less inhibited, and will not play down the severe strains which an energy crisis implies for capitalism today. But their own social project will not escape a similar critique, unless it has at least the basic outline of a solution to the problem — unless it can point to the satisfactions it envisages as replacing the dubious rewards of the commodity culture.

One project which sketches such a solution is that of self-managed socialism. The substitution of the principle of self-management for the present dominant principle of hierarchy in every walk of life — a substitution possible only if the power of the capitalist is overthrown and that of the bureaucrat severely limited at least — implies on the level of the individual, the possibility of changing the values one lives by. If new channels of self-expression and autonomous action can be opened up in every social sphere, beginning with the factory floor, it will not be so crushing a catastrophe if beer must be brought in bottles rather than in energy-expensive aluminium cans.

This point has been made in greater detail elsewhere.[41] It illustrates how the campaign against nuclear power must be finally unconvincing, unless it is prepared to delineate an alternative social path, a credible one that does not lead to a poisoned world. A receptive atmosphere for such an exposition is created by the striking irrationality of the nuclear programme, which must condemn by association the system that gives rise to it, and encourage the consideration of rational alternatives.

FOOTNOTES

1. Discussed in *The Closing Circle*, by Barry Commoner, Jonathan Cape 1972.

2. "Nuclear Electric Power", by David J. Rose, page 359. *Science, 184* 19 April 1974.

3. *Nuclear News*, April 1975, p.80. (The ruling Swedish Social Democrats subsequently lost the general election in which their remaining plans for nuclear plants were severely challenged.)

4. *Nuclear News*, April 1975, p.33 (editorial).

5. The best source here is *Non-nuclear futures*, by Amory B. Lovins and John H. Price (Ballinger Publishing Company, Cambridge Mass.), October 1975, which contains an encyclopaedic list of references.

6. *Nature, 253*, p.385 (February 6, 1975, editorial).

7. *Investir*, March 24 1975. Quoted in Basquet, *Le Nouvel Observateur*, April 21 1975, p.46.

8. For the latter two incidents, see respectively *Environment, 16*, October 1974, page 21, and *Time*, September 22 1975 ("Fromme: 'There is a Gun Pointed'").

9. "The Hidden Commitment of Nuclear Wastes", by W.D. Rowe and W.F. Holcomb. *Nuclear Technology, 24*, December 1974, p.286.

10. "Plutonium Recycle: The Fateful Step", by J.G. Speth, A.R. Tamplin and T.B. Cochran. *Bulletin of the Atomic Scientists*, November 1974, page 19.

11. *Ibid.*, page 20.

12. *New Scientist*, March 27 1975, page 799.

13. A 1000 Megawatt (electrical) reactor requires about 4,500 tons of uranium over its lifetime. Thus a world total of 2,000 reactors (one of the lower estimates) by 2000 AD would need some 9 million tons; but the estimated world inventory extractable at less than $39 a kilogram is 4 million tons. (See e.g. "World Uranium Resources", by L.G. Poole, *Nuclear Engineering International*, February 1975).

14. See the discussion in Speth *et.al* (ref.10 above).

15. See e.g. "A Troublesome Brew", by Sheldon Novick, and "A Poor Buy", by T.B. Cochran *et.al*, both in *Environment, 17*, June 1975.

16. "The Deflation of Rancho Seco 2", by Jim Harding. Reprinted from *Not Man Apart* (undated).

17. *Alternatives au nucléaire,* Presses universitaires de Grenoble, February 1975. The figure cited follows from Annexe 3, page 89, on utilising the findings on capital cost from ref.18 below, and those on capacity factor from ref.19 below.

18. "The Economics of Nuclear Power", by I.C. Bupp and J.C. Derian *et.al. Technology Review,* February 1975.

19. "Will Idle Capacity Kill Nuclear Power?" by D.D. Comey. *Bulletin of the Atomic Scientists,* November 1974.

20. In Part 2 ("Dynamic Energy Analysis and Nuclear Power") of *Non-nuclear Futures,* by A.B. Lovins and J.H. Price. Ballinger (Cambridge Mass.), 1975.

21. *Nuclear Engineering International,* February 1975, page 73.

22. *Le Nouvel Observateur,* April 28, 1975, page 86.

23. "The World Energy Market", by B.C. Netschert, *Bulletin of the Atomic Scientists,* October 1971.

24. *New Scientist,* August 17 1972, page 334.

25. *Nuclear Engineering International,* September 1974, page 741.

26. *Nuclear Engineering International,* May 1975, page 451.

27. "The Failsafe Risk", by Kurt H. Hokenemser. *Environment 17,* January/February 1975.

28. *New Scientist,* June 26 1975, page 710.

29. "A Poor Buy", op.cit., page 12.

30. *The Case for Solar Energy,* by Peter E. Glaser. Arthur D. Little Inc., Cambridge, Mass., 1972.

31. "The Ecological Crisis of Consumerism", by Alan Roberts, *International,* September 1973: "Crise Écologique et Soviété de Consommation", *Sous le Drapeau du Socialisme,* nos.60 and 61, 1973.

32. *Nuclear Engineering International,* May 1975, p.447.

33. *Nuclear Engineering International,* April 1975, p.301.

34. "The Nuclear Backlash", by Michael Kenward. *New Scientist,* May 1975.

35. *Nuclear Engineering International,* September 1974, p.743.

36. "World List of Nuclear Power Plants", *Nuclear News,* August 1975, p.63.

37. "Radioactive Waste Management in Selected Foreign

Countries", by H.M. Parker. *Nuclear Technology, 24,* December 1974, page 307.

38. "Review of the impact of production and use of energy on the environment and the role of UNEP", by the United Nations Environment Programme, no.75-40793, 1975.

39. See *Nuclear Engineering International:* "Market considerations of medium/small nuclear power reactors", by J. Greason (page 37), and "The case for developing small power reactors", by G. Webb (page 39), both January 1974; "IAEA General Conference asks why no small reactors for developing countries?"

40. "A Critique of Political Ecology", by Hans-Magnus Enzensberger, *New Left Review* No.84, March-April 1974.

41. *"Consumerism" and the Ecological Crisis,* by Alan Roberts, Spokesman Pamphlet No.43, 1974.

Nuclear Disaster
in the Soviet Union*

Zhores Medvedev

In my article "Two decades of dissidence" (*New Scientist*, vol.72, p.264), I mentioned the occurrence at the end of 1957 or beginning of 1958 of a nuclear disaster in the southern Urals. I described how the disaster had resulted from a sudden explosion involving nuclear waste stored in underground shelters, not far from where the first Soviet military reactors had been built; how strong winds carried a mixture of radioactive products and soil over a large area, probably more than a thousand square miles in size; and how many villages and small towns were not evacuated on time, probably causing the deaths later of several hundred people from radiation sickness.

I was unaware at the time that this nuclear disaster was absolutely unknown to Western experts, and my *New Scientist* article created an unexpected sensation. Reports about this 20-year-old nuclear disaster appeared in almost all the major newspapers. At the same time, some Western nuclear experts, including the chairman of the United Kingdom Atomic Energy Authority, Sir John

*First published in the *New Scientist*, 30 June 1977, to whom grateful acknowledgement is made.

Hill, tried to dismiss my story as "science-fiction", "rubbish" or a "figment of the imagination".

However, about a month later my story was confirmed by Professor Lev Tumerman, former head of the biophysics laboratory at the Institute of Molecular Biology in Moscow, who had emigrated to Israel in 1972. Tumerman visited the area between the two Ural cities — Cheliabinsk and Sverdlovsk — in 1960. He was able to see that hundreds of square miles of land there had been so heavily contaminated by radioactive wastes that the area was forbidden territory. All the villages and small towns had been destroyed so as to make the dangerous zone uninhabitable and to prevent the evacuated people from returning. Tumerman's eye-witness evidence did not, however, convince all the experts, including Sir John Hill, of the truth of this disaster. Doubts remained that the story was exaggerated. These doubts convinced me of the need to collect more information that would throw light on the real scale of this nuclear disaster.

Different kinds of nuclear accidents release different kinds of radioactive products into the environment. If *reactor nuclear waste* is scattered from a storage area the result will be quite specific. The numerous short-lived radioactive isotopes, with very intensive gamma and beta radiation, will already have disappeared during the storage period. Only long-lived isotopes, which constitute about 5 to 6 per cent of the initial radioactivity, remain dangerous after the first two or three months. Radioactive strontium-90 and caesium-137 are the

most important of these. Both have half-lives of about 30 years. Caesium-137, as an isotope with gamma radiation, is more dangerous for external irradiation. However, it is less cumulative and, because it is more soluble and is not fixed permanently in biological structures, it disappears more rapidly from animals and the soil. Strontium-90 is a close analogue of calcium and is able to substitute for calcium in both bones and soil. Since calcium forms part of permanent body structure, this means that strontium-90 can be fixed in animals for many years, while it may remain for hundreds of years in the soil. This is why strontium-90, which emits beta radiation, is considered the most dangerous product from nuclear bomb tests and the nuclear industry.

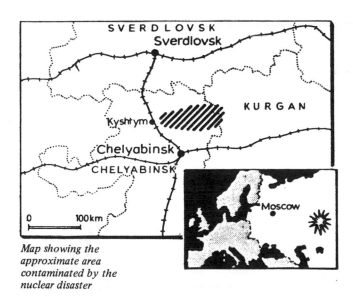

Map showing the approximate area contaminated by the nuclear disaster

If the nuclear disaster in the Urals really caused the contamination of hundreds or thousands of square miles of territory, this area must still be polluted today — heavily by strontium-90, and partly by caesium-137. The soil, soil animals, plants, insects, mammals, lakes, fish and all other forms of life in this area would still contain significant amounts of strontium-90 and caesium-137. The random distribution of radioactive isotopes during an accident of this type would cause the isotope concentration level to vary enormously from place to place. In many areas the external and internal radiation would seriously threaten the life of many species — increasing their mutation load and mortality, and inducing many other changes. The extremely large contaminated area would also create a unique community of animals and plants, where genetic, population, botanical, zoological and limnological research into the influence of radioactive contamination could be studied in its natural conditions.

Critics of Tumerman's and my story can obviously ask: why then did Soviet scientists miss this chance to study the unique radiobiological and genetic problems, which this enormous (certainly the largest in the world) radioactive environment provided for long-term study?

The answer is very simple — the Soviet scientists *did not miss this chance*. More than 100 works on the effect of strontium-90 and caesium-137 in natural plant and animal populations have been published since 1958. In most of these publications, neither the cause nor the geographical location of the contaminated area are indicated. This is the unavoidable price of censorship. However, the specific composition of the plants and animals, the climate, soil types and many other indicators leads to the inevitable conclusion that it lies in the south Urals. (In one publication, the Cheliabinsk region is actually mentioned — a censorship slip.) The terms of observation — 10 years in 1968, 11 in 1969, 14

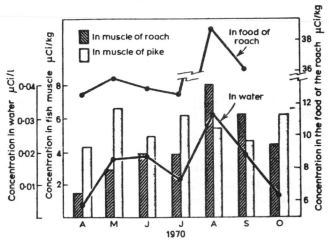

Variations in the concentration of caesium-137 — based on the research of A.I. Il'enko

in 1971, and so on — reveal the approximate date of the original accident. Finally, the scale of the research (especially with mammals, birds and fish) indicates clearly that rather heavy radioactive contamination covered hundreds of square miles of an area containing several large lakes.

I had known about the nuclear waste explosion in the Urals since 1958. My professor at that time, Vsevolod Klechkovsky, who was a leading expert in the use of radioactive isotopes and radiation in agricultural research, was given the job of setting up an experimental station within the contaminated territory. The station was to study the effect of radioactive isotopes on plant and animal life and to monitor the so-called "secondary distribution" of the contamination. Radioactive pollution of this type cannot be confined within the initial area, since soil erosion and biological distribution constantly widen the radioactive region. The specific activity of the contamination declines with time both in the original area and the new neighbouring ones. Klechkovsky offered me a job at this station, but I did not accept it as the work was classified. A number of junior researchers from his department of agrochemistry and biochemistry at the Timiriazev Agricultural Academy, however, did go to work there, and still do today.

At the beginning all work associated with this nuclear disaster was considered as highly classified. There was no chance of publishing any research results. The situation changed slightly after Krushchev's demise, because blame could then be laid on the nuclear authorities appointed by him. The chairman of the State Committee for Atomic Energy of the USSR, Professor Vasily Emelyanov, was dismissed from his post in 1965; some other high officials in both the peaceful and military branches of the atomic energy industry went as well.

It was too late in 1965/1966, and it was considered unnecessary, to acknowledge the catastrophe that had taken place years before. But at least the high level of secrecy which had surrounded the disaster was lifted. Many experts from the

Soviet Academy of Sciences and other research establishments were allowed to start comprehensive research in the contaminated area and to publish their results in Soviet academic journals. The ending of Lysenko's domination in biology and genetics also helped this change in attitude. Several new research institutes and units specialising in genetics, radiobology and ecology, set up in 1965 and 1966, pressed hard for access to this unique radioactive environment.

These studies started, unfortunately, several years *after* the initial impact of the radioactive hazard on the community which comprised all levels of life — from soil bacteria through to large animals, plants and trees. Farm animals and plants, as well as the human population, were included in places of "secondary distribution" where the radioactivity level had not been so high as to force evacuation.

One of the first works that pointed to a possible serious industrial nuclear disaster was published in 1966 (see *Atomnaya Energiya,* vol.18, p.379). At first glance the paper appeared to be purely mathematical. Its title — "The calculation method for the distribution of radioactive contamination in water and bottom deposits of non-running water lakes" — was rather theoretical, and the whole text was saturated with mathematical equations. This study was based on measurements that had been taken in two lakes contaminated by industrial radioactive waste five years previously. (Since the paper had been submitted for publication in May, 1964, the work must have been completed some

time in 1963.) The author, F. Rovinsky, found
tha the isotope composition was complex at first,
but after the first few months strontium-90 became dominant. The water radioactivity (the level
in absolute figures was not given) fell quickly
during the first two years because of the absorption
by the silt. Then some kind of equilibrium was
established between the bottom silt deposits and
the water. The theoretical calculations and the
experimental picture were almost identical. One
can find hardly anything wrong with the whole
work or the "experimental contamination", except
for the size of the two lakes referred to. "The experimental lakes were", wrote Rovinsky, "eutrophic
types, the first was 11.3 sq.km in size and the
second was 4.5 sq.km, both almost round in
shape." It is rather hard to believe that anyone in
his right mind would contaminate two such large
lakes just to confirm some mathematical calculations. However, I did not find any other research
on these two particular lakes.

A third contaminated lake appeared in two
papers by A.I. Il'enko, published at the beginning
of the 1970s (see *Voprosy Ichtiologii,* vol.10,
p.1127; vol.12, p.174). Il'enko had studied the
distribution of caesium-137 and strontium-90 in
water, plankton, water plants, and different species
of fish between 1968 and 1970, but the lake had
been contaminated many years before. He gave the
actual isotope concentration of both isotopes in
this lake. It varied every month depending very
much on seasonal conditions, and with maximum
peaks during October and July. Such variations

could only be typical of a running water lake with a contaminated basin. During the summer of 1969, the concentration of strontium-90 in the water was 0.2 microcurie per litre (μ Ci/l.), and that of caesium-137 was 0.025 μ Ci/l. Both figures are 100 times higher than contamination levels in ponds created specifically for research purposes, both in the USSR and other countries.

A lake with 50,000,000 curies

The purpose of Il'enko's work was to study food chains among different forms of life in the lake. Pike were the largest and final link in the chain. Il'enko had measured the isotope concentration in the bones and muscle of more than 100 pike, some weighing as much as 25 to 30 lbs. The lake was not a rich one, since only four species of fish were found there. And as it is important for food chain studies that the population balance is not seriously affected, the number of pike in the lake must have been at least 10 to 20 times the number studied. A lake containing this number of large pike must be between 10 to 20 square kilometres in size. One would need at least 50,000 Ci to contaminate such a lake with strontium-90 up to the level of 0.2 Ci/l, that is if it were non-running and not too deep. For a running water lake the amount would have to be much greater. But in either case such a level of radioactivity is far too high to handle for experimental purposes.

The lakes in the Urals region usually have very thick bottom silt deposits. The total amount of strontium-90 in the bottom silt of the two lakes which Rovinsky studied was at least 10 times higher than in the water, once equilibrium was reached. However, these were non-running-water type lakes. The lake studied by Il'enko, had an intensive turnover of its water supply — the strontium-90 concentration could vary up or down by more than 400 per cent within one month. These conditions meant that the bottom silt and the water plants became the main accumulators of radioactive materials — a process which had started many years before Il'enko's experiments. Il'enko calculated that the total amount of caesium-137 and strontium-90 in the water plants, plankton and silt was about *1000 times higher than in the water*. For example, the concentration of caesium-137 in water plants varied from 10 to 38 μCi/kg.

This means that the total minimum amount of strontium-90 and caesium-137 in the whole lake must be around 50 million curies. And this enormous amount of radioactivity filtered into the lake from the lake's basin! It is well known that soil fixes strontium very strongly, so only a small fraction could have filtered through with the soil water — probably some five to six per cent over several years.

It is, of course, impossible to know precisely how many hundreds of millions of curies of strontium-90 and caesium-137 would have to be fixed in its basin for such an enormous amount of radioactivity to accumulate in a running water lake. There are no precedents for such research. This radioactivity is equivalent to thousands of tons of radium. Could anyone imagine that this amount of radioactive material would be distributed over the area surrounding the lake, just for "experimental" purposes?

Many papers have been published on the different species living in the contaminated area. The levels of soil contamination were usually the same with the different experiments — from 0.2 to 1.0, from 1.0 to 1.5 and from 1.8 to 3.4 mCi of strontium-90, and 4.0 to 7.0 μ Ci of caesium-137 per square metre between 1965 and 1969. Il'enko and his collaborators also carried out several studies of mammals *at the same time* as they were doing their work on the lake's population, between 1968 and 1970. Since the samples of fish and animals were taken continuously, the whole research was certainly carried out in the same environment. In two studies of mammals, where food chains were also the main research aim about 2000 individual animals from 15 different species were killed (see *Zoologicheskii Zhurnal*, vol.49, p.1370; *Zhurnal Obschei Biologii*, vol.31, p.698). Small animals, such as mice, rats and rabbits, are poor indicators of the size of a research area. However, these two papers reported killing 21 deer from the contaminated area. This final link of the food chain is indeed rather revealing. Since the shooting had to be done without causing any serious depletion in the natural population or species ratios, at least 100 deer must have been available. Deer migrate normally over large distances, especially during winter, so the area covered should have been at least 100 square miles.

The level of soil contamination by strontium-90,

of between 1.8 and 3.4 mCi/sq.m, is also much higher than any possible "experimental" contamination. About one million curies of strontium-90 would be necessary to obtain such an "experimental" field.

Works by other authors, in which the plants, soils and soil animals were studied, also indicated an area on a geographical scale, not just a fenced-off field. Their identical levels of radioactivity and cross references to Il'enko's work indicate that it was in fact the same "experimental" area these authors were studying. The contaminated territory had many different soil types, consisting as it did of meadows, hills, plains and various kinds of forests. In general, within any contamination area there were at least six or seven ecological groups.

A large research team, headed by academician N.P. Dubinin, has carried out work on the population genetics of the area — the frequency and pattern of chromosomal aberrations, comparative radio-sensitivity, selection of radio-resistant forms, and so on. It is clear that they were working in the same contaminated area as the one used for the other studies. The authors refer to Il'enko's work when quoting the level of radioactivity as being 1.8 to 3.4 and 1.0 to 1.5 mCi/sq.m. They also acknowledge that the area was not contaminated on purpose for their experiments, and that they had only been able to start their radiobiological and genetical observations *seven years after the organisms, selected for research purposes, had already been living in the radioactive environment* (see *Uspekhi Sovremennoi Genetiki,* vol.4, p.170).

This lapse of time was a definite research disadvantage. The early adaptation stages had been missed and the initial level of irradiation by the mixture of short-lived and long-lived isotopes was unknown. Despite these methodical aberrations, the authors were able to find a selection of more resistant forms and some other genetical population changes in soil algae (chlorella), many plants (mostly perennial), and rodents, particularly species of mice.

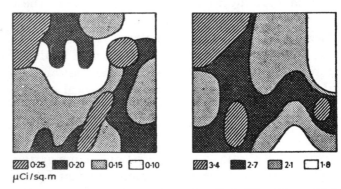

///// 0·25   ■■■ 0·20   ▓▓▓ 0·15   ☐ 0·10
µCi/sq.m

///// 3·4   ■■■ 2·7   ▓▓▓ 2·1   ☐ 1·8

Left: *average concentration of strontium-90 (,uCi/g of dry weight) in plants in a section of the contaminated area; and* right: *contamination of the soil with strontium-90 (,uCi/sq.m) – based on the work of A.I. Il'enko in 1967. The distributions are random and therefore probably accidental*

The special aspect of the work, which I wish to emphasise here, is the size of the research area. For example, the research team started their work on rodents with a population that had *already lived 30 generations in a radioactive environment*. One has to be certain for population genetics work that the individual animals being used for the different measurements are the true ancestors of those animals which lived in the area when the original radioactive contamination occurred. Rodents do not migrate very far during their adult life, perhaps about 1000 metres. However, with each new generation the migration from the ancestral environment will be even further. During 30 generations, migration could reach as much as 20 to 30 kilometres, which means 400 to 900 square kilometres of radioactive environment. Dubinin and his colleagues do not give the exact size of their research area, but they do admit that all the animals they studied had really lived in the radioactive zone over all these years.

Single-cell soil algae (chlorella) are extremely resistant to radioactive contamination, so their level of genetical damage should be much higher than for those species which just could not survive. Dubinin and his team took samples of chlorella some five years, or 200 generations after the radioactive contamination had occurred. The work was clearly carried out in a different area, one perhaps where only the algae could have survived. The radioactivity of the soil was much higher, its maximum activity being 10^{10} disintegrations per kilogramme of soil per minute. This activity calculated per square metre is about five curies for a surface layer of 8 to 10 cm depth!

There was a very uneven distribution of radioactive contamination over the area used for this research. The work that has been published on plants and animals was carried out in places where these animals and plants could live for many generations. Other areas, where they were not able to survive, were certainly not explored so thoroughly. But the existence of such areas in this general geographical location has been acknowledged by Dubinin. In his autobiography, *Vechnoe Dvizhenie*, he describes how his group carried out long-term research in an area "contaminated by high doses of radioactive substances" where "some members of the species have died out, some are suffering and declining slowly, while others have evolved a higher resistance".

The nature of the plant and animal species refer- red to in these research papers — there are more than 200 species in all — can easily indicate the approximate geographical location of the area under study. The mixture of European and Siberian species points to the Urals. This conclusion is con- firmed by the accidental acknowledgements in one of the recent works of Il'enko and his collaborators that *the animals for their work had been collected in the Cheliabinsk region.* This particular research was done during the autumn of 1971 and the animals had been living in a radioactive environ- ment for 14 years — in other words since the autumn of 1957.

The papers, that I have referred to, represent only a small fraction of the research data that has been published on this contaminated environ- ment in different Soviet scientific journals. The nuclear authorities in Britain and the US probably put more trust in the expensive information they receive from monitoring global fall-out or from space-satellite surveillance. They certainly do not read such Soviet journals as *Voprosy Ichtiologii,*